ONe WORLD, MANY PeOPLe

For dear Riley -
Welcome to "One World
Many People"
And experience
"precious love
Past"
Please pen me a note F
tell me how you have
enjoyed this book.
Annette Parrott MA Ba
2008

ONE WORLD, MANY PEOPLE

Anthropology Made Fun for Kids

An Illustrated Text and Activity Guide

ANNETTE BARNETT, MA Ed

Illustrated by Isa Barnett

YOUNG
SCHOLARS
PRESS

Santa Fe, New Mexico

Published by: Young Scholars Press
354 1/2 Calle Loma Norte
Santa Fe, NM 87501
www.oneworldmanypeople.com

Editor: Ellen Kleiner
Book design and production: Janice St. Marie

Printed in China by South China Printing Co., Ltd.

Publisher's Cataloging-in-Publication Data

Barnett, Annette.

One world, many people : anthropology made fun for kids : an illustrated textbook and activity guide / Annette Barnett ; illustrations by Isa Barnett. -- 1st ed. -- Santa Fe, N.M. : Young Scholars Press, 2006.

p. ; cm.
ISBN-13: 978-0-9787138-0-5
ISBN-10: 0-9787138-0-X
Includes glossary and bibliographic references.
Audience: elementary grades.
Summary: Introduces the idea that human beings everywhere have the same needs, which we fulfill in various ways depending on the materials available to us. Through short chapters followed by a series of activities, students learn to identify with essential human conditions, apply their imaginations as their ancestors did, and appreciate the diverse cultural weave that gives meaning and purpose to present-day life.

1. Anthropology--Juvenile literature. 2. Ethnology--Juvenile literature. 3. Anthropology--Study and teaching--Juvenile literature. 4. Ethnology--Study and teaching--Juvenile literature. I. Barnett, Isa. II. Title.

GN31.5 .B37   2006 2006905853
301/0834 --dc22   0610

To my late husband Isa,
who taught me how to expand my universe of artistic possibilities
and without whose support this labor of love would not have been possible ~

You were a vast storehouse of knowledge and a masterful artist.
May your song and genius continue to guide those you loved
as you parley with heavenly beings.

ACKNOWLEDGMENTS

Many of the ideas in this book were first conceived by my son Stephen Barnett, to whom I am deeply thankful.

To my teachers throughout the decades—especially Susan Morris, Karen Cook, Maria Chapis, Leslie Clifton, Sheelagh Clark, Carol Woltering, Shirley Chalick, Karen Ambruso, Marion Galante, and Doris Mitrani—I owe pages of gratitude for the wisdom and dedication you skillfully showered upon me.

I wish to thank Thery Giger, legendary administrator of the school where this material was first introduced, for her many gifts.

Special indebtedness to Alejandro Lopez, a brilliant multicultural educator, editor, and advisor, whose tireless dedication to this text has been invaluable, and whose knowledge and insight will be a lasting inspiration to me.

Thanks as well to Bill Oliver, Ron Spicer, Charlie Fifer, and Jack Crane, master artists who came to my rescue and completed the necessary renderings with sensitivity and a heightened aesthetic sense.

To my dear friends in Santa Fe, New Mexico—Mary Lawton, Kerry Brock, and Shelly Fullmer—with love for editing the manuscript in its early stages.

To Dina Wolf Bloomberg and Janice Barnett, with love and appreciation for taking time to edit the developed manuscript.

To my dear friend Dr. Eliot Gould, for being so supportive and instrumental in showing me how to digitize the text. He is a precious gift to me.

I would also like to express my indebtedness to my award-winning editor, Ellen Kleiner, who made complex choices to achieve perfection in this rendering while conveying my passionate belief in young people, and to Janice St. Marie, a gifted graphic designer with a critical eye, for distinctive ways of adding beauty and color to the pages of this book.

And finally, to my precious students, I am grateful for your unconditional love and laughter. That is how I will see you forever.

CONTENTS

FOREWORD

One World, Many People is an outgrowth of the holistic teaching principles and practices employed for many years at Ms. Annette's Creative Nursery & Kindergarten in suburban Philadelphia. One of the hallmarks of this renowned school was the uncomplicated richness and sophistication of what children learned there. On a typical morning, children learned to count in a foreign language on an abacus or with blue corn kernels, or they improvised a ballet to the music of Brahms, waving colored scarves in the air; hours later, they kneaded bread or made corn-husk dolls.

Once a week, the children were visited by anthropologist-in-residence Stephen Barnett. Under his tutelage, they learned about humankind's achievements in tools and technology, agriculture, clothing, shelter, and transportation. They listened attentively to his captivating stories about how people lived in various parts of the world, the resources they used, and the artifacts they made. He brought them examples of stone tools, African masks, vintage bottles, musical instruments, and Native American moccasins, among many other things.

In keeping with the educational philosophy of the school, the children got the chance not only to handle these artifacts but also to extend their knowledge by creating their own simple versions of them. In a short time, the children had amassed enough artifacts to establish their own compelling "Living Museum of Cultural Anthropology."

Few experiences during the week, regardless of their richness of content, could evoke the joy and wonder with which children embraced Stephen's Anthropology for Kids course. And with good reason, for amidst the vast storehouse of human knowledge few stories are as compelling as that of the rise of human civilization from the discovery of fire to the launching of space rockets. This story, however well understood and recounted by historians, scientists, and anthropologists, contains many unknowns and is steeped in the mystery that while we are many people of various times and cultures, we are all parts of one world.

For children who are born into our present time of extreme complexity and copious material output, this simple-to-use book will serve as a clear road map for maneuvering through it. Page after page, children will learn that regardless of the changes occurring all around them, human life remains irrevocably rooted in procuring the essentials of food, shelter, clothing, and all that brings comfort, beauty, meaning, and wonder to our lives. Children, the most recent recipients of both the most ancient and the most novel human traditions, are sure to appreciate learning about their priceless history.

—Alejandro Lopez, Multicultural Educator
University of New Mexico

INTRODUCTION

This book introduces school-age children to anthropology, the study of human beings and their material culture. Although the subject matter is usually reserved for adults, young people who explore it do so with a seemingly insatiable curiosity to learn about human discoveries and inventions around the world. In gaining an understanding of other cultures, they develop new insights into their own.

Anthropologists tell us that our earliest ancestors lived in trees in east Africa and survived by eating fruits and nuts. They say that the weather changed and the trees began to disappear, leaving only grasslands. As a result, human beings learned to walk upright and their bodies stretched so they could see beyond the tall grasses. Then eventually, from that place in Africa, early human beings migrated to every continent of the earth.

To survive, they, like the animals around them, required food, shelter, and protection against predators and the cold. But while animals could dig in the earth, run very fast or fly through the air, camouflage themselves against predators or grow thick fur for defense against the cold, human beings could not. They solved the challenges of survival instead by making things—objects we now call artifacts. In some places, artifacts of even the earliest known human species, named *Homo habilis* (human beings who made primitive stone tools), have survived to this day. To create these and other life-saving objects, nature provided them, and us, with an opposable thumb and infinite imagination.

One World, Many People traces the latest concepts in anthropology across cultures and throughout time. The text focuses on three core human expressions: the survival arts, the functional arts, and the ritual, recreational, and decorative arts. An activity guide following the text invites teachers and parents to engage children in hands-on tasks that reinforce the knowledge imparted in the text. The book concludes with a glossary of anthropological terms to help make their meanings clear to young readers. It is my hope that educators, parents, and others engaged in a holistic approach to children's academic development welcome this addition to their collection of literature.

UNIT 1

THE SURVIVAL ARTS

Artifacts

Food

Shelter

Clothing

Bags and Containers

Tools

Transportation

Child's Hide
Moccasins

San Blas
Doll

Mexican
Mask

Zuni
Turquoise
Brooch

Unglazed
Prehistoric
Pottery

Chinese
Bronze
Ladle

Child's
Rawhide
Parfleche

ARTIFACTS

Artifacts are material things we use in everyday life. Your toothbrush and school supplies are small artifacts. A canoe, bicycle, and farm equipment are large artifacts.

We study artifacts to understand similarities and differences among societies around the world. Anthropologists, who study human beings and their material culture, know that people of long ago, no matter where they lived, made material things for everyday use, and not for display. Some made tents for shelter; others built rickshaws for travel; and still others crafted cups to hold water and hats for warmth.

Over the last twenty-five years, changes in technology have led to manufactured artifacts that are much more powerful than the handmade or tool-made artifacts of the past. The computer and cell phone, for example, help us communicate with one another and assist us in our work. They also free us up, giving parents more time to play with their children and everyone more time to learn about the world. And while there is a vast difference between a computer and an abacus, their purpose is the same. In fact, the roots of most of today's artifacts can be seen in the simpler forms used in the past.

What artifacts do you use in school and at home?

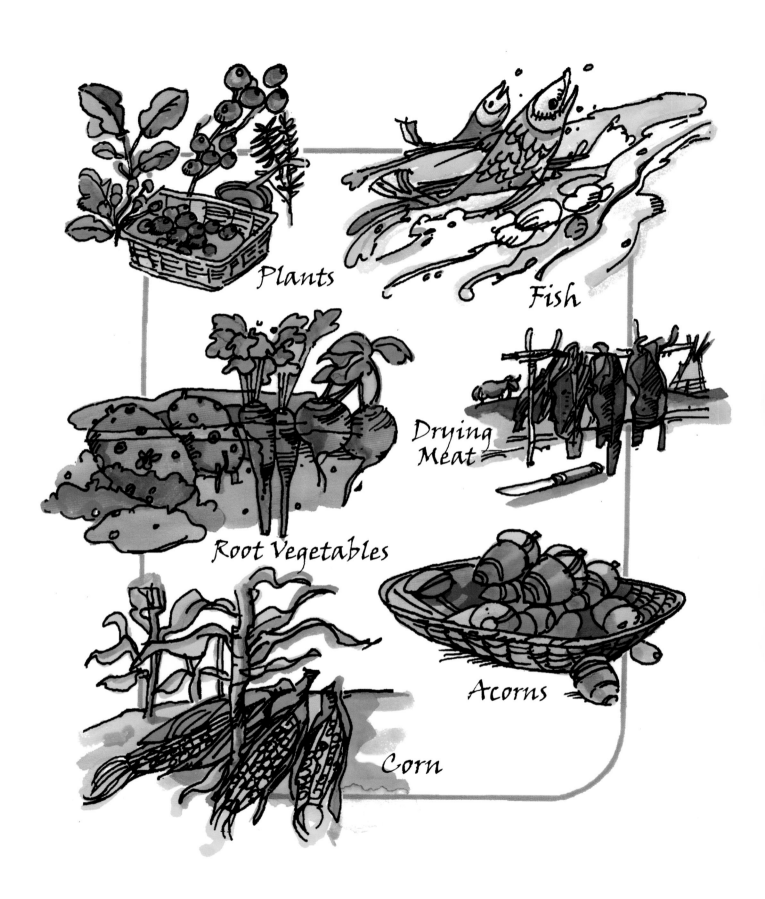

Plants

Fish

Root Vegetables

Drying Meat

Corn

Acorns

FOOD

Thousands of years ago, our ancestors survived by eating foods that grew in the wild. The women, for the most part, gathered seeds, berries and other fruits, roots, and nuts in baskets. The men made bows, arrows, spears, and harpoons, which they used to hunt buffalo, bear, deer, elk, gazelle, turtle, rabbit, or fish, depending on where they lived. These men and women were called hunters and gatherers.

Over time, people in many parts of the world learned to ensure a steady food supply by growing their own fruits and grains. In China, families planted rice. In the Americas, Native cultures grew corn. In the Middle East and Europe, villagers cultivated wheat, and in Africa, millet. These people were all called farmers.

To make sure there would be food in times of need, farmers also kept animals in pens near their homes or herded them in fields close by. The animals—especially chickens, pigs, sheep, and goats—soon became tamed, or domesticated. The growing and raising of such animals and other food to eat is known as agriculture.

Today, most families go to the supermarket to buy agricultural products like fruits, vegetables, grains, nuts, meat, and fish. Much of this food was grown on large farms or in hatcheries hundreds or thousands of miles away. It was then packaged for freshness and transported to the supermarket by jet, boat, train, or truck.

What foods, if any, have you grown in a garden?

Tepee

Brick House

Wigwam

Igloo

Log Cabin

False Front

SHELTER

From the beginning of time, human survival depended on the ability to find shelter from cold, heat, rain, wind, snow, and wildlife. At first, our ancestors took shelter in caves or treetops. Later, often working together, they built more durable homes to live in.

Throughout the world, people built homes from materials they found in nature. In places that were extremely cold and snowy, they used blocks of ice to build igloos. Where there were animals like buffalo or reindeer, they used hides to make tepees and other shelters. Where there was an abundance of trees, they used logs to build cabins, huts, or lodges.

In areas that lacked these materials, people built homes of stone. Or they mixed sandy soil with water and straw to make sun-dried bricks for adobe houses.

Today, people live in homes of stone, cement, wood, brick, glass, metal, or other materials. In some parts of the world, friends and neighbors still get together to build houses for one another, while in other parts architects design homes and construction companies hire crews to build them.

What materials is your home made of, and who built it?

Mexico

Russia

Arctic

Africa

South
Pacific

Japan

CLOTHING

The clothing our ancestors wore had a lot to do with the weather in their part of the world—if it was hot or cold, wet or dry. People of the Ice Age were probably the first to wear clothes to keep warm. These were made from the hides of buffalo, bear, elk, moose, and other large animals they hunted, skinned, and tanned. Once the skins were soft and pliable, several were sewn together with animal sinew and made into clothing. The animals' bones were the first needles.

Later, people learned how to weave cloth from various fibers, using a simple device called a loom. On the loom, fibers twisted into thread were interlocked with one another. Common materials interlocked to make clothing included sheep's wool (an animal fiber) and cotton (a plant fiber). A woman in China began making fine threads of silk from the protein fiber silkworms excrete while making their cocoons.

In our modern age, power-driven looms weave fabric from wool, cotton, and silk. Fabric today is also made from synthetic fibers such as rayon, nylon, and polyester, which come from chemicals and petroleum. Once the cloth is made, seamstresses and tailors use large machines to sew it into pants, shirts, dresses, or other articles of clothing.

What kinds of fibers are your clothes made from?

Baskets

Bottles

Bucket

Lunchbox

Parfleche

BAGS AND CONTAINERS

Of the many types of bags and containers used throughout history, woven baskets were among the first. These baskets, made to hold water, seeds, and other food items, were woven from twigs and plant fibers. The idea for creating baskets in this way came from watching birds make nests from similar materials.

Another early type of container was the Native American parfleche, used for storing and transporting food, clothing, tools, building supplies, and other items necessary for survival. Crafted of stiff dried hide in rectangular shapes, these were sometimes made in matching pairs and used as saddlebags. At other times they were shaped as cylinders and then painted.

Later, European cultures developed glass by melting then quickly cooling sand and other minerals. Roman glass, for instance, was often blown into the shape of bottles for holding medicine or perfume, and sealed with a small stone. Other bottles held liquids such as water, oil, or wine.

Today, we use a wide assortment of containers. Farmers everywhere rely on strong wooden buckets or galvanized metal pails for hauling and storing milk, water, and animal feed. People worldwide also use cardboard boxes, paper bags, tin cans, aluminum flasks, plastic packaging, and kitchenware that is leakproof, unbreakable, insulated, and even collapsible.

When you go to school, what kind of container do you carry your lunch in?

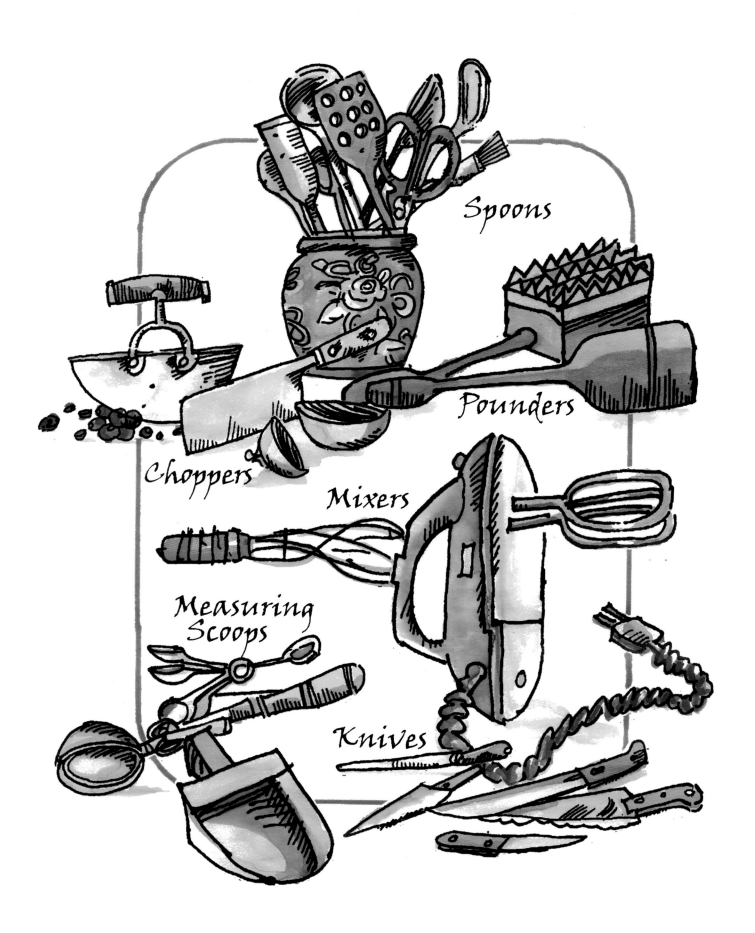

Spoons

Pounders

Choppers

Mixers

Measuring
Scoops

Knives

TOOLS

Human beings' first tools were their hands. But the work of survival was difficult, and to make it easier they developed more specialized tools. It is likely that chimpanzees too used tools, mainly the versatile digging stick. People not only sharpened sticks for digging but also flattened stone points for chipping and fractured animal bones and antlers for scraping, sewing, and other tasks.

To help them hunt for food, they shaped wooden clubs, spears, and bows and arrows. Next came stone axes, choppers, and knives.

Today, we live in a world powered by electricity, fossil fuels, and wind and solar energy. Stone, wood, and iron have given way to durable plastics and other highly technological materials. Also, tools operated by human strength have been replaced by machine-driven devices like computers, calculators, power saws, lawn mowers, glue guns, electric mixers, and a wide range of medical and carpentry equipment. We even have tools that record the weather on distant planets.

How does your favorite tool work?

TRANSPORTATION

For most of human history, people walked to the places they needed to get to. They walked to the hunting grounds, sometimes traveling for days over steep hills and through streambeds, gathering nuts, berries, and other fruits along the way. Or they hiked long distances carrying heavy loads on their backs to market, making pilgrimages, or visiting friends.

Human beings soon found they could ride animals instead, such as camels, donkeys, horses, or elephants. Sometimes they would ride in special carts, wagons, or sleds pulled by mules, horses, or even teams of dogs. Using these forms of transportation, they could travel farther and carry more items.

People who lived near water made rafts, canoes, larger boats, or ships to transport villagers, food, and artifacts to other places. To propel the vessels through the water, they designed paddles, sails, and engines.

Over the last two hundred years, many kinds of machines were invented to carry human beings across longer distances in less time. Today, we have everything from bicycles, motorcycles, and cars to trains, buses, planes, and space shuttles. We even have skateboards.

What is your favorite form of transportation, and why?

UNIT 2

THE FUNCTIONAL ARTS

Pottery

Animal Skins

Weights and Measures

Musical Instruments

Writing

Money

Taos Pueblo in New Mexico

Pueblo Pottery

POTTERY

Once our ancestors had mastered the arts of survival, they directed much of their attention to the functional arts, especially pottery, the shaping and firing of clayware. Clay, an abundant material made of the finest particles of earth, could be found almost anywhere. Pliable and flexible, it was molded into various forms, particularly round ones.

Pottery was first discovered when baskets lined with soft clay to hold water accidentally came in contact with fire. The fire hardened the clay into a stonelike substance that could withstand high temperatures and hold water for longer periods of time. Soon, vessels made of clay were used for cooking and serving food as well as for carrying and storing water.

One of the earliest traditions of pottery making arose in China. Earthenware pots were also made in the Middle East, Africa, Europe, and the Americas. All these cultures created their pottery by hand, using either a coil or thumb-pinch method.

Among Pueblo Indians of the Southwestern United States, the creation of a traditional pot was, and still is, a sacred activity. First, the potter asks permission to take clay from the earth. After the pot is formed, a design is painted on its surface as a way of asking for rain, fertility, or good crops. The completed pot is then baked in an open pit with cow manure and later smothered with horse manure to hold in the smoke and blacken the surfaces.

What functional artifacts have you made out of clay?

Bearskin

Doeskin
Quiver

Ladies' Hide
Moccasins

Indian Doll
Deerskin
Wampum
Necklace

ANIMAL SKINS

Animal skins were invaluable to early human beings. Whether thick and furry or thin and watertight, they could be wrapped around the body to keep heat in and cold out, or to protect against rain, snow, and ice.

Hunters in search of animal skins killed big and small game alike—buffalo, bear, elk, deer, mountain sheep, fox, rabbit, and squirrel—and skinned it using stone or obsidian knives and scrapers. To make the skins soft and pliable, they tanned them with special substances. The best substances were the animals' brains, which were often wrapped in the skins and buried in the ground for a period of time.

Once removed from the ground, the tanned animal skins were sewn into dresses, shirts, leggings, moccasins, jackets, and robes, as well as blankets, pouches, and lodges or tepees. After being stitched together with bone needles and animal sinew, many items were beaded, quilled, or adorned with pieces of bone, antlers, and animal tails.

People today still like the warmth and water-resistance of clothing made from animal skins. In addition to the types of garments our ancestors dressed in, we also wear leather jackets, belts, boots, hats, gloves, and fur coats. And instead of carrying pouches we use leather handbags.

Which of your clothes are made from animal skins?

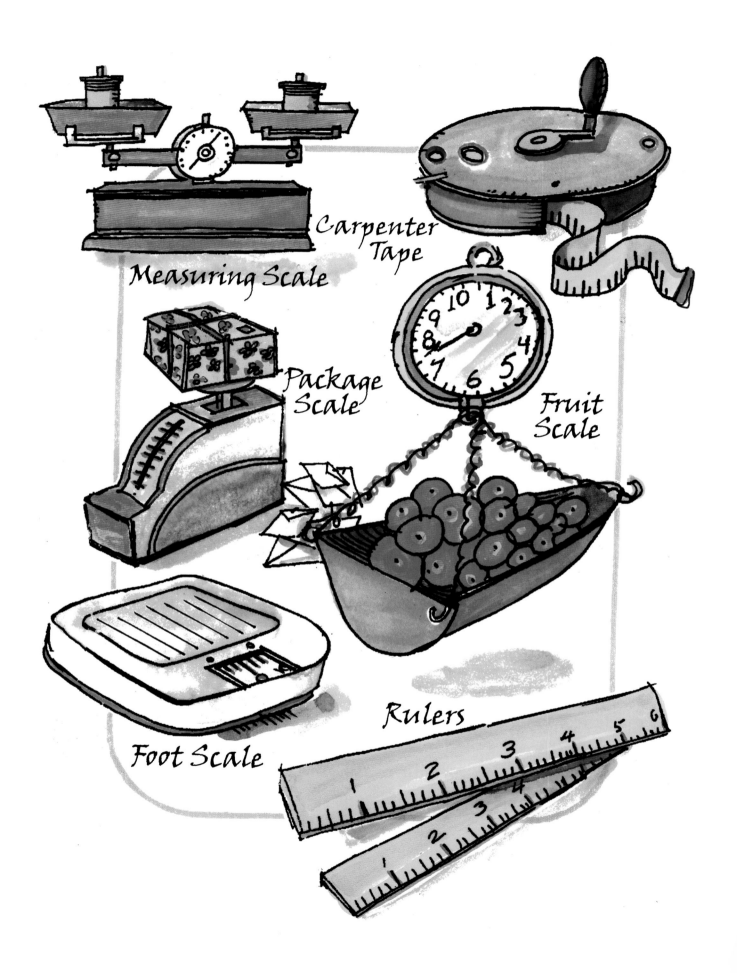

Measuring Scale

Carpenter Tape

Package Scale

Fruit Scale

Foot Scale

Rulers

WEIGHTS AND MEASURES

Over thousands of years, human beings have devised many ways to weigh and measure things in their world. Early on, they designed scales to weigh grains, fruits, vegetables, fish, and precious metals. To measure size and distance, they used the length of an arm, the spread of a hand, or the span of a human foot or a piece of stringlike material.

Ancient Egyptians were the first people to develop precise drafting instruments. With these they quantified not only objects within their reach but also the movement of heavenly bodies, a science now known as astronomy. Precisely measuring the movement of the sun, moon, and stars allowed them to mark the passing of days, months, and years. Later, these direct observations of heavenly bodies were replaced by clocks, hourglasses, and calendars.

In the fifteenth century, the Ashanti tribe of West Africa invented a method for weighing gold dust. They placed it on a scale with little brass weights they had cast through the lost-wax process.

Present-day instruments for determining weights and measures are much more refined. Pharmacists weigh medicines in milligrams, a tiny fraction of the smallest unit of weight. Chefs and family cooks use measuring spoons and cups. Carpenters use retractable rulers. And today we measure not only weight, size, and distance, but also temperature, pressure, and speed.

What do you learn when you step on a scale, use a ruler, or look at your wristwatch?

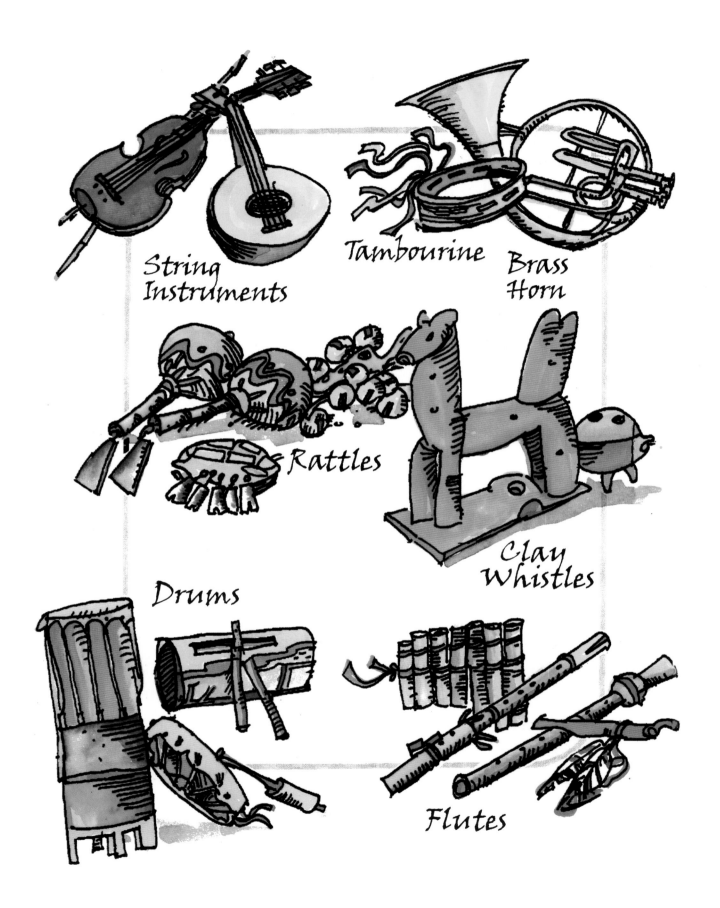

String
Instruments

Tambourine

Brass
Horn

Rattles

Clay
Whistles

Drums

Flutes

MUSICAL INSTRUMENTS

At first, human beings used their powerful bodies to create musical sounds. They would clap hands together in a group, slap the side of the body, stamp the feet, whistle, and sometimes chant. Today, tribesmen in the highlands of Papua, New Guinea, still come out of the bush by foot, in full traditional dress, for their annual "sing sing," in which their voices relay their feelings toward one another.

In addition to using their bodies, people throughout the world began expressing themselves also through musical instruments made of bone, clay, wood and animal sinew, metal, or other available materials. Some cultures made simple flutes, bagpipes, or harmonicas to blow into, all of which are called wind instruments. Others crafted early forms of harps, guitars, or violins, made of tightly pulled strings that vibrated when plucked or rubbed, and are known as string instruments. People of nearly all cultures made drums, bells, rattles, tambourines, and cymbals to strike or shake, which are called percussion instruments.

Modern-day musical instruments are sometimes more complex, like the piano—a keyboard instrument—or the piccolo, trombone, saxophone, bassoon, double bass, chimes, marimbas, and even spoons. Despite this diversity, and even electronic novelties such as the Moog synthesizer, today's large symphony orchestras are made up of the three major instrument types long known to humanity: wind, string, and percussion instruments.

What feelings can you convey by making sounds with your hands and feet?

Chinese
Characters

Pre-Columbian
Script

Cave
Painting

Sumerian
Tablet

Egyptian
Hieroglyphs

WRITING

One of human beings' greatest needs is to communicate—to share stories, ideas, and feelings with one another. At first, our ancestors communicated through spoken words. Later, they discovered that drawing pictures on rock walls or tree bark helped them record, or remember ("keep a memory" of), certain things, such as animals they had killed or amounts of grain they had stored for the winter. Through picture writing, people also conveyed information to others.

As time went on, cultures of the Far East and Southwestern Asia began writing scripts with markings instead of pictures. In early China, people etched their scripts on animal bones, while Sumerians impressed theirs on wet clay tablets. Ancient Egyptians, too, developed a system of script writing, as did the Maya and Aztec Indians of the Americas and the Phoenicians of the Middle East. The Phoenician alphabet evolved into the script we use today, in which sounds are combined to form words and the words are arranged into sentences and paragraphs.

Hundreds of years ago, people wrote their scripts using pointed bird feathers or crow quills for pens, and ink made from colorful parts of plants—walnut shells for brown, and flowers for yellow and blue. Pen-and-ink writing was eventually replaced by movable block type and printing presses that could turn out thousands of books, newspapers, or magazines at once. Today, a computer disk can store more information than a set of encyclopedias. And while some people still write letters by hand, many communicate only through e-mail.

What special messages do you like to convey through writing?

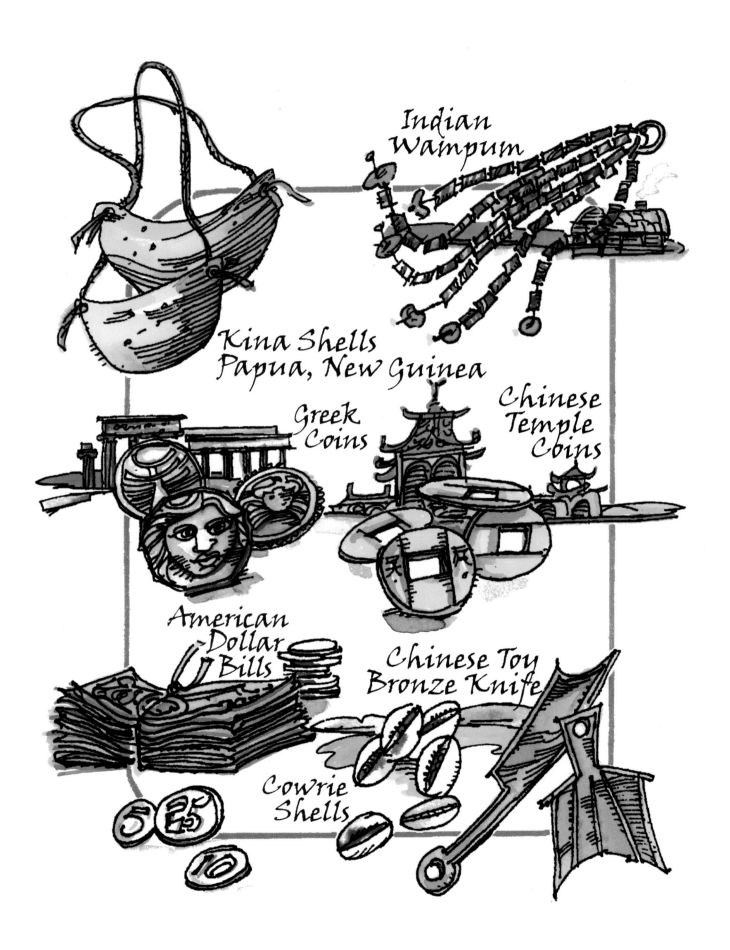

Indian Wampum

Kina Shells
Papua, New Guinea

Greek Coins

Chinese Temple Coins

American Dollar Bills

Chinese Toy Bronze Knife

Cowrie Shells

MONEY

Thousands of years before the invention of paper dollars, money consisted of shells, beads, or pieces of clay tablets. People in Oceanic societies traded long strips of woven string decorated with cowrie shells for food and other necessities. To meet their survival needs, African villagers traded beads. Later, Plains Indians of America traded buffalo hides, Arizona's Pima Indians traded cotton, and Northwestern tribes traveled miles every year carrying fish and clams—all to exchange for items that would ensure their survival.

As time passed, people in China, Greece, Europe, and eventually the Americas began using gold and silver coins as currency. Now, instead of exchanging one item for another, human beings were spending money of a certain value to buy things worth that same value. Today, nearly everywhere in the world, coins, paper bills, and credit cards are presented in exchange for goods and services.

And still money is changing to meet human needs. On January 1, 2002, Western Europeans established a universal currency, the Euro, replacing many of the national currencies they were used to. Now the official currency of the European Union, the euro provides neighboring countries with money that has a common design, value system, name, and symbol (€) which makes buying and selling easier for everyone.

When someone gives you money, what do you use it for?

UNIT 3

THe RiTUAL, ReCReATiONAL, AND DeCORATiVe ARTS

Masks

Dolls

Toys

Games

Design and Decoration

African

Iroquois

New Guinean

MASKS

Along with the functional and survival arts, early human beings took part in ritual, recreational, and decorative arts. One of the earliest ritual arts was the practice of deception, or hiding one's identity behind a mask. Wearing a mask was also a way of absorbing the power of the person, animal, or force it represented.

Masks have helped to shape cultures everywhere—from Greece to Africa and the South Pacific, from Indonesia to China and Japan, and the Americas as well. Ancient Greeks used masks in their plays to represent gods, goddesses, and the forces of fate. They also created masks of comedy and tragedy that came to symbolize drama. In West Africa, masks were, and still are, worn by doctors attempting to drive sickness from their patients.

Seneca Indians of central New York state wore masks in hopes of growing good crops. Their masks were made from corn husks, which they braided into coils to form the shape of a face. Members of the Husk Face Society who wore these masks were known as Bushyheads.

Today, masks are worn on stage, in parades, and for other dramatic events. During Halloween, for example, young people wear masks to hide their faces and briefly take on the identity of someone else.

How do you feel while wearing a mask?

Plains Doll

Corn-Husk Doll

Barbie Doll

Porcelain Doll

Colonial Doll

Raggedy Andy

Puppet Doll

Kachina Dolls

DOLLS

Dolls have always been dearly loved, especially by children, who carry them, dress them, and tell them their deepest secrets. Dolls of long ago were fashioned from materials as varied as clay, sealskin, palm leaves, apple heads, corn husks, wood, and deerskin. But it is their clothing that tells us where they were made.

Dolls draped in rebozos, shawls long enough to cradle a sleeping child, are usually made in Mexico. Dolls in long velveteen dresses, with gold sequins, beaded necklaces, earrings, and low buckskin boots are created by Navajo women in Arizona and New Mexico. The women themselves wear this traditional style of clothing.

During colonial times in America, wealthy parents had dolls from England shipped to their daughters. The dolls' faces were made of precious porcelain, their eyes of glass, and they had human hair. Because these dolls were too valuable to play with, the girls made their own out of scraps of old dresses and sheets.

Other cultures view dolls as more than playthings or showcase items. The Hopi and Zuni tribes of the Southwestern United States say the cottonwood kachina dolls they carve have good spirits that help people. In fact, dancers wearing masks often believe they themselves have become kachinas.

Everywhere, dolls continue to win over the imagination. New types include dolls of ethnic origin, which reflect not only the clothing but also the physical features of the people who made them.

If you ever had a favorite doll, what was it made of?

TOYS

Our ancestors loved to play with toys. Among the few surviving artifacts from the distant past, toys have been found the world over, indicating they were as common long ago as they are today. Those that survived—tiny stone axes, pottery animals and dolls, basketry, miniature bows and arrows, buckskin and corn-husk dolls—were made from durable materials.

The very first toys, however, were sticks, stones, shells, chunks of clay, and animal bones. As time passed, parents added special features to these materials, turning them into small human or animal figures, or miniature replicas of everyday objects.

Toys, like all artifacts, reflect the local culture. Inuit children living in the Arctic were given tiny dog-sleds to play with. Young Chinese children were given kites, while older ones designed and made their own.

In modern times, children almost everywhere enjoy playing with blocks, toy boats, cars, trains, trucks, motorcycles, and an assortment of action figures resembling people, animals, or space creatures. Allowing their imaginations to soar, they create castles, towers, bridges, and roads. Favorite toys, many of which reflect today's expanding use of materials, include plastic models, sock or papier-mâché puppets, electronic video games, and Barbie doll accessories like trunks for her clothes and carriages for wheeling her around.

What is your favorite toy, and what is it made of?

Discus

Hoop Ball

Lacrosse

Baseball

Skateboarding

Running

Games

The very earliest human beings challenged their abilities by playing games requiring physical dexterity. The most common ones involved running, chasing balls or other objects, and throwing sticks.

These activities inspired a multitude of games in cultures throughout the world, each one making use of local materials. The Tarahumara Indians of northwestern Mexico chased wooden balls, made from oak or other tree roots, at breakneck speeds. Woodland Indians of eastern Canada threw snow-snakes, special sticks about six feet long that could take eight years to shape and harden, down icy tracks of snow. Both games are still played today.

In modern society, numerous games remain organized around the use of a ball or throwing stick. Ball games include baseball, basketball, hockey, football, soccer, volleyball, lacrosse, and also golf, table tennis, and billiards. Games involving the tossing of sticks have developed into archery and javelin throwing. People also toss sticks to outguess chance while gambling. Cards, dice, and many board games share this goal.

What are your favorite games, and why do you enjoy them?

Face
Decoration

Basket

Wooden Horse

Gourd

Shirt

Pottery

DESIGN AND DECORATION

Human beings of long ago were avid designers. They decorated their shelters, clothing, and other artifacts by either painting, carving, etching, sewing, or incising them on one or more surfaces. Some designs illustrated events or the artist's thoughts or beliefs; others were for protection or beauty.

Early Europeans used clay pigments and animal fat to decorate cave walls with images of deer and bison. In the Southwestern United States, Native peoples carved petroglyphs on hard stone surfaces, while those in the Pacific Northwest carved symbols on totem poles. All these designs gave expression to the culture's myths, creation stories, and understanding of how the world works.

As human beings around the world discovered additional resources, their designs came to expression through different materials. In the Middle East, people began inlaying silver jewelry with precious stones or making finely tooled leathers. In Africa, they applied bold batik designs to fabric and geometric designs to the walls of their homes.

Here in the United States, communities known as the "Plain People," or Amish, make some of today's most ornately designed quilts. Museums and collectors alike treasure the refined handiwork, with its brilliantly colored diamonds, stars, strips, and floral designs.

What designs would you choose for decorating your bedroom, and what materials would you use?

ACTIVITY GUIDE

The activities that follow are for teachers and parents to introduce to young readers. Each is a hands-on project designed to deepen the child's inner sense of the conditions early human beings faced in the world they inhabited. In the process, it awakens an appreciation for the various cultural adaptations that came later, including present-day inventions.

Every activity corresponds with a topic presented in the text and can be completed fairly quickly with the adult's help. *Please note:* there is no activity listed for the section entitled "Artifacts," because the outcome of each project is itself a future artifact.

THE SURVIVAL ARTS

FOOD

HISTORIC APPLICATION: The wandering hunters dwelling north, east, and west of the American Plains came from every part of the country. Tribes such as Blackfoot, Arapaho, and Cheyenne had moved out from the eastern woodlands, leaving their cornfields and pottery kilns to trade for horses and begin a new life as Plains Indians. Considering that to primitive people wealth is expressed not in money but in food, these hunters were some of the richest Indians in America. The buffalo, especially their vitamin-rich internal organs, gave food in abundance, and hundredweights of it sun-dried as jerky could be kept for months. Pounded fine and mixed with fat and dried berries, it formed a staple known as pemmican.

PRESENT-DAY APPLICATION: Make peanut butter using 5 ounces of peanuts and 2 tablespoons of cooking oil. Combine ingredients in a blender, and grind peanuts to a smooth consistency. Serve on crackers and enjoy!

MATERIALS NEEDED: Blender, peanuts, cooking oil, spoon or plastic knife, and crackers. (For children allergic to peanuts, substitute 5 ounces of almonds or another nut or seed.)

SHELTER

HISTORIC APPLICATION: One early type of shelter is a simple lean-to, made of poles and cloth to keep out the cold. Lean-tos were very common in frontier America.

PRESENT-DAY APPLICATION: Draw a model for a lean-to. Using thick dowels or tree saplings for the poles, construct the lean-to in your classroom or backyard. Or go camping with your classmates and build your lean-to on the campgrounds.

MATERIALS NEEDED: A large sheet of paper, colored pencils, several thick dowels or 4-inch tree saplings, 2 yards of heavy cloth, paints to decorate the cloth, masking tape, and glue.

CLOTHING

HISTORIC APPLICATION: The type of place where people lived—hot or cold, wet or dry—had a lot to do with the kind of clothing they wore. People of the Ice Age wore fur skins sewn together with animal sinew.

PRESENT-DAY APPLICATION: Create a poncho by starting out with a large rectangle of available cloth. To make an opening for the head, cut a hole with a diameter of 10 inches at the center. Using the scissors once again, fringe the bottom.

MATERIALS NEEDED: Cloth, scissors, ruler, and marking pen.

BAGS AND CONTAINERS

HISTORIC APPLICATION: Woven baskets were among the first types of containers used for holding water, seeds, and similar items. Other types of containers, especially in warm climates, were large leaves or palm fronds, which early humans took with them while gathering food.

PRESENT-DAY APPLICATION: Holding a large leaf of carefully washed romaine lettuce, spread a layer of cream cheese or vegetable dip on top, wrap, and eat.

MATERIALS NEEDED: Romaine lettuce, plastic knife, and cream cheese or vegetable dip.

TOOLS

HISTORIC APPLICATION: Various tools were made for cutting up food, skinning animals, and shaping other tools. Eskimo stone hammerheads, found with bone and ivory handles, were probably the earliest multipurpose tools. Stone hammerheads remain in general use.

PRESENT-DAY APPLICATION: Make your own tapping hammer. Find a sturdy forked tree branch to use as a handle, place a flat hard oval stone in the fork, and wrap it tightly in place with rawhide or heavy cord.

MATERIALS NEEDED: A sturdy branch, a flat hard stone, rawhide or heavy cord.

TRANSPORTATION

HISTORIC APPLICATION: For most of human history, people walked to places they needed to go. But it was no easy matter for Native Americans to follow buffalo on foot with only dogs to carry their baggage for them. To carry more things, they constructed a travois, a cart with a seat made of willow saplings and a frame made of poles wrapped in nonslip buckskin. These were dragged either by hand, by harness on the shoulders of the traveler, or by one or two harnessed dogs or horses.

PRESENT-DAY APPLICATION: Working as a team with your classmates, build a scaled-down version of a travois. For the vertical section of the frame, wrap two sticks or poles with hide. For the horizontal cross section to hold the supplies, wrap 1-inch dowels or tree saplings with rawhide and, using heavy cord or more rawhide, secure the travois to the poles.

MATERIALS NEEDED: 2 sticks or poles, rawhide, 1-inch dowels or tree saplings, and heavy cord.

travois

THE FUNCTIONAL ARTS

POTTERY

HISTORIC APPLICATION: The hardness of clay and its capacity to hold water made pottery suitable for cooking among many early cultures.

PRESENT-DAY APPLICATION: Although cookware is now made of cast iron or stainless steel in most parts of the world, many households still use pottery to serve and store food and water. To make a small clay pot, warm a ball of clay with your hands, roll it into a coil, then wind the coil into a continuous base and up into a circular wall. Pinch the various levels of the coil together, and smooth the interior and exterior walls. Using a stick, draw designs on the wet clay surfaces. Finally, fire the pot in a pottery kiln, or your home or school oven, at 500 degrees Fahrenheit.

MATERIALS NEEDED: Moist soft clay, a narrow pointed stick, and access to an electric kiln or an oven.

ANIMAL SKINS

HISTORIC APPLICATION: For thousands of years, human beings hunted large game animals, taking their meat for food and their skins for clothing. First, they made the skins soft by tanning them; then, using bone needles and animal sinew, they sewed pieces of the tanned hide into garments.

PRESENT-DAY APPLICATION: Create a simple leather bracelet by selecting a strip of buckskin 3 inches wide and long enough to overlap the wrist for easy removal, allowing enough at the bottom to be cut into thin strips of fringe. Cut the ends of the fringe at a slant to create points for easy stringing. Punch several holes along the top of the buckskin. To secure the bracelet, thread each strip of fringe through its corresponding hole then knot it. Slip colorful beads on the end of each strip, knotting it again to hold them in place.

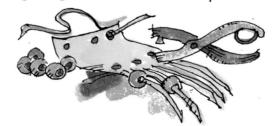

MATERIALS NEEDED: Buckskin, pony beads, and a hole punch. (These materials can be obtained at a local hobby shop or through a crafts catalog.)

WEIGHTS AND MEASURES

HISTORIC APPLICATION: Most ancient cultures devised ways to weigh and measure ordinary objects. In the more recent past, a piece of string as long as an arm, the spread of a hand, or the span of a foot was used to measure distance and size.

PRESENT-DAY APPLICATION: Weigh yourself on a scale. Using a tape measure, see how tall you are. Record both numbers, then weigh and measure yourself again next month to see if you have grown.

MATERIALS NEEDED: Weighing scale, tape measure, pencil, and paper.

MUSICAL INSTRUMENTS

HISTORIC APPLICATION: Early human beings worldwide played musical instruments, especially percussion instruments. In many parts of the world, gourds were harvested, dried, and, with the seeds remaining inside, used as dance rattles.

PRESENT-DAY APPLICATION: A large cylindrical oatmeal box is perfect for making a percussion instrument known as an African talking drum. Stretch heavy parchment paper or leather over each open end of the box and extending about 1 inch beyond the circumference for a drumhead. Wrap and tie the drumheads in place with heavy cord or rawhide.

MATERIALS NEEDED: Large oatmeal box, heavy parchment paper or leather, and heavy cord or rawhide.

INDIAN WAMPUM

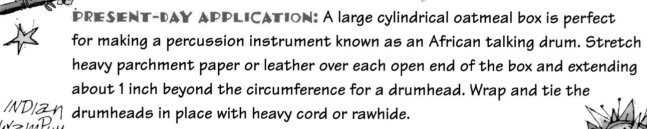

Temple COINS

China

WRITING

HISTORIC APPLICATION: The discovery of clay tablets containing cuneiform script reveals that historically writing was actually a form of symbolic storytelling. Each little picture in the script was a symbol standing for something in the world. These tablets, with their symbols, have been called silent witnesses to the remains of early Sumerian temples.

PRESENT-DAY APPLICATION: Write a story using symbols instead of words. For examples of symbols already in use, study road or recreation signs.

MATERIALS NEEDED: Paper and colored pencils, or markers. Use examples of traffic or recreation signs that convey a message to motorists.

MONEY

HISTORIC APPLICATION: In many places around the world, coins made of gold or silver came to be used as currency for buying things.

PRESENT-DAY APPLICATION: Design the front and back of a coin to illustrate an important event or person in recent history. To begin, sketch a few ideas on tracing paper. Transfer your favorite one to a 7-inch circle cut from poster board. Highlight the name of the person or event in silver or gold.

MATERIALS NEEDED: Colored pencils, tracing paper, poster board, a compass, and a gold or silver magic marker.

THE RITUAL, RECREATIONAL, AND DECORATIVE ARTS

MASKS

HISTORIC APPLICATION: Masks, the most spectacular article used in ceremonies around the world, were often worn to honor the local gods and spirits. At ceremonial dances, participants with their faces concealed would sing and dance, shake rattles, and beat their drums. Masks of the Northwest Coast Indians were sometimes grotesque and oversized, while those worn by Greek actors were small, exotic, and hand held.

PRESENT-DAY APPLICATION: In *The Lion King*, a stage play, the actors wear convincing masks that make them look like lions. To make a convincing mask of your own, choose a character from a storybook. Using paper and colored markers, design a mask that will make you look like this character. Copy the mask onto poster board. Cut it out, punch holes on either side, draw a lace through the holes, and knot the ends. Cut holes for the eyes, paint the mask, and decorate it by attaching assorted materials.

MATERIALS NEEDED: Paper, colored markers, poster board, scissors, hole punch, a lace (thin leather cord), paint, paintbrush, glue, strips of leather, cloth, ribbon, sequins, buttons, colored tissue paper, feathers, ribbons, and other trimmings.

DOLLS

HISTORIC APPLICATION: For thousands of years, people interested in doll making used materials they found in their immediate surroundings—cloth, wood, corn husks, fur, hair, leather, beads, metal, and more. Many of these dolls were dressed to resemble the people who made them.

PRESENT-DAY APPLICATION: Create a corn-husk doll with modern accents. Stack 4 large corn husks on top of one another and fold the stack, top to bottom, at the center. Tie a piece of heavy string or yarn about 1 inch below the fold to make the head. Roll another husk lengthwise for the arms, forming the hands by tying the husk about 1 inch from each end. Pass this husk through the other husks, just below the first tie, so the arms reach out from the body. Attach materials for the hair. Finally, add a necklace made of uniquely shaped macaroni that has been laced together on a cord.

MATERIALS NEEDED: Corn husks (available at craft stores or in the Mexican food section of your grocery store), heavy string or yarn, scissors, corn silk (or moss, yarn, or wool), macaroni, and a lace (thin leather cord).

TOYS

HISTORIC APPLICATION: History, in the form of old toys, tells us there was much love and affection for children around the world. Toys have survived the passage of time because of their durable materials, as in the case of ivory birds, pottery animals and dolls, and basketry cradles.

PRESENT-DAY APPLICATION: Before the invention of plastic in the twentieth century, most toys in the United States were carefully crafted from wood. Gather a few examples of antique and modern-day wooden toys, and demonstrate how they might have been made.

MATERIALS NEEDED: Wooden toys arranged in a large circle for discussion.

GAMES

HISTORIC APPLICATION: Games in early times required little or no special equipment or setup time, and were played by children of all ages. One popular game in America's colonial era involved rolling a metal hoop (from a wooden barrel) along the ground by running behind it and guiding its direction with a stick. Children, each rolling their own hoop, would race one another, working hard to maintain control of their hoop over rough ground.

PRESENT-DAY APPLICATION: Create a hoop roll of your own on the playground, using a large plastic hoop and a wooden spoon or ruler.

MATERIALS NEEDED: Plastic hoop, and a wooden spoon or ruler.

DESIGN AND DECORATION

HISTORIC APPLICATION: Human beings in every part of the world have expressed their artistic aspirations through folk art, often by painting, carving, etching, sewing, or incising images on objects. Some of the earliest people decorated their caves, using clay pigments and animal fat.

PRESENT-DAY APPLICATION: Decorate your classroom or bedroom using bold designs cut out from folded colored paper. String the shapes together and suspend them from the walls or ceiling.

MATERIALS NEEDED: Colored paper, scissors, and masking tape.

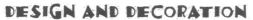

Glossary

adobe. Sun-dried mud bricks used to construct homes in arid regions of the world.

agriculture. The practice of growing food to eat.

Amish. Pertaining to a strict Mennonite sect that settled in North America during the eighteenth century.

anthropology. The study of human beings and their material culture.

artifacts. Objects made and used by human beings.

astronomy. The study of celestial bodies such as planets and stars.

bagpipe. A wind instrument consisting of a leather bag, a valve-stopped tube, and three or four pipes.

batik. An Indonesian method of hand-printing textiles by using wax to coat parts not to be dyed.

block-type printing. Printing from carved wooden blocks.

Bushyheads. Members of the Husk Face society of the Seneca Indian people of present-day New York state.

cowrie shells. The glossy casings of small warm-sea snails.

cuneiform. A writing system used by ancient Sumerians, in which they impressed wedge-shaped symbols on wet clay that they then baked.

currency. Any kind of money used as payment for something.

cylindrical. The shape of a long, round, solid or hollow object domesticate. To tame something that was once wild.

dwelling. A shelter.

environment. Surrounding conditions or forces that influence people, plants, and animals.

etch. To impress something sharply or clearly.

ethnic. Pertaining to races or large groups of people sharing common traits or customs.

euro. A recent currency devised to circulate in many countries of Europe.

fertile. Fruitful or prolific.

fiber. A thread or slender root.

fire. To subject dry clay items to intense heat in order to harden them.

fossil fuel. A combustible substance, such as coal, oil, or gas, produced from the remains of past plant or animal life that has been preserved in the earth's crust.

fringe. An ornamental border consisting of short straight or twisted threads hanging from cut or raveled edges of a cloth.

geometric. Pertaining to lines and shapes.

gods. Beings thought to possess more-than-human power.

grotesque. Decorative art featuring distorted human and animal forms interwoven with foliage.

hammerhead. The striking part of a hammer.

harness. Gear used to fasten a cart to a draft animal.

harpoon. A barbed spear used especially in hunting large fish or whales.

Homo habilis. The first human species, who made primitive stone tools.

Ice Age. A period of widespread glaciation occurring from 1.8 million to 10,000 years ago and known as the Pleistocene age.

incise. To cut into or engrave.

gatherers. People who provided their own food by harvesting available seeds, berries and other fruits, roots, and nuts.

hundredweight. A unit of weight equal to a hundred pounds.

igloo. An Inuit shelter made of blocks of ice.

Inuit. A north Alaskan Indian tribe that made its living by hunting and fishing.

kachina. A wooden hand-painted doll of the Pueblo Indian tribes of Arizona and New Mexico, used to represent certain forces of nature.

lean-to. A basic shelter with three walls and a sloping roof.

leggings. Protective leg coverings usually made of hide or cloth.

lodge. A house set apart for a special purpose or use during a particular season or for particular people.

lost-wax process. An ancient practice still in widespread use, by which liquid metal solidifying in a mold replaces a wax model, turning soft clay sculptures into a harder material such as bronze.

machine. A device made of several parts that transmits force, motion, and energy to accomplish a desired goal.

measure. To mark in specific multiples of a unit.

millet. A small-seeded cereal forage grass that grows annually.

obsidian. Natural glass formed by the cooling of molten lava.

Oceanic. Pertaining to the island cultures of Oceania, or the South Pacific.

palm fronds. The long broad leaves of a palm tree.

parchment paper. Paper made to resemble the skin of a sheep or goat, and prepared to serve as a writing surface.

parfleche. A rectangular dried-hide container made by Plains Indians of the United States.

pemmican. A paste of dried pounded meat, nuts, and berries used by Northeastern and Plains Indians of the United States.

petroglyph. A picture or symbol pecked into stone with another stone.

Plain People. Amish men, women, and children of the Eastern United States.

poncho. A protective cloth covering with a central hole for the head, worn by men in Mexico.

pony beads. Large-holed beads of brilliant color.

rebozo. A sometimes fringed rectangular cloth worn by Mexican women.

rickshaw. A cart used in the Far East for transporting one or two passengers and pulled by another person.

script. A written text.

sinew. A cord or thread usually made from the tendon of an animal.

Sumerian. Pertaining to the people of ancient Sumer, in Mesopotamia.

symphonic. Harmonious sounds associated with a symphony orchestra.

talking drum. An hourglass-shaped African drum used to relay messages between people or communities, often during ceremonies.

tepee. A conical tent usually made of skins and used by Native Americans.

thatch. A plant material (as straw) used for roofing.

traditions. Information, beliefs, or customs handed down from one generation to another.

travois. A vehicle consisting of two trailing poles bearing a platform or cart for the load, used by Plains Indians of the United States.

BIBLIOGRAPHY

Broder, Patricia Janice. *Hopi Painting*. New York: E. P. Dutton, 1978.

Cameron, E. L. *Isn't S-H-E a Doll?* Oakland, Calif.: Regents of University of California, 1996.

Carlson, Laurie. *Colonial Kids*. Chicago: Chicago Review Press, 1997.

Der Manuelian, Peter. *Hieroglyphs from A to Z*. Boston: Boston Museum of Fine Arts, 1999.

Donoughue, Carol. *The Mystery of the Hieroglyphs*. New York: Oxford University Press, 1999.

Glubok, Shirley. *The Art of the North American Indian*. New York: Harper & Row, 1964.

Hofsinde, Robert. *The Indian and the Buffalo*. New York: William Morrow, 1961.

Kraft, Herbert C. *The Lenape or Delaware Indians*. South Orange, N.J.: Seton Hall University Museum, 1991.

McGregor, J. C. *The Cohonia Culture of Northwestern Arizona*. Urbana, Ill.: The University of Illinois Press, 1951.

Miles, Charles. *Indian and Eskimo Artifacts of North America*. Chicago: Henry Regency Company, 1963.

Newmann, Dana. *Ready-to-Use Activities and Materials on Desert Indians*. New York: The Center for Applied Research Education, 1995.

Shannon, Helen, and Hazel Ulseth. *Antique Children's Fashions, 1880–1900*. Cumberland, Md.: Hobby House Press, 1982.

Smith, Shelley J., Jeanne M. Moe, Kelly A. Letts, and Danielle M. Patterson. *Intrigue of the Past.* Washington, D.C.: Cultural Heritage Education Program, Bureau of Land Management, 1996.

Sullivan, Michael. *The Arts of China.* Berkeley, Calif.: University of California Press, 1967.

Underhill, Ruth Murray. *Red Man's America.* Chicago: University of Chicago Press, 1967.

White, Joyce C. *Ban Chiang Discovery of a Lost Bronze Age.* Philadelphia: The University Museum, University of Pennsylvania, 1982.

Wilkinson, Phil, ed. *Early Humans.* New York: Alfred A. Knopf, 1989.

ABOUT THE AUTHOR

Annette Barnett, MA Ed., a renowned arts educator, has long been a pioneer in early childhood education. Ms. Annette's Creative Nursery & Kindergarten, the Philadelphia-based school she founded and directed for more than three decades, was one of the first preschools admitted to the United Private Academic Schools Association and an incubator for progressive multicultural education in the United States. She also served as a visiting arts instructor at the Loretto Heights College in Denver, Colorado, and at the Children's Museum in Santa Fe, New Mexico. More recently, she worked as a visiting artist at Santa Fe's Georgia O'Keeffe Museum.

In addition, Ms. Barnett taught at the Santa Fe Community College, where she presented her hallmark course, Anthropology for Kids, and was appointed by the Bureau of Indian Affairs to develop standards of excellence for curriculum development and teacher training. A presenter at child development conventions of the National Association for the Education of Young Children as well, she participated in Harvard University's Kennedy School of Government forum on *Brown v. the Board of Education*.

Ms. Barnett received her Master of Art Education degree from the University of the Arts in Philadelphia, where she was awarded the Sylvia Wexler Prize, and subsequently graduated from the prestigious Barnes Foundation in Merion, Pennsylvania, upon completing her study of the educational philosophy of John Dewey. She currently lives in Santa Fe, New Mexico, where she directs the Northern Pueblos Literacy Project.

ABOUT THE ILLUSTRATOR

Like Bert Phillips, Ernest Blumenschein, and other artists before him, Isa Barnett (1923–2001), prominent illustrator and painter, migrated from the East Coast to the Southwest. Captivated by the light and culture of Santa Fe, he established a home and studio there in addition to those in his hometown of Media, Pennsylvania.

Barnett's studies began at Fleisher Art School and the Philadelphia Museum College of Art. Following military service in World War II, he combined teaching and freelance work, creating illustrations for such publications as *The Saturday Evening Post, Argosy, Life, American Heritage,* and *Reader's Digest.* In 1964, following a commission from the Morrel Ham Company in Chicago for twelve paintings depicting the life of Abraham Lincoln, his work traveled to the New York World's Fair. In 1968, paintings he produced while touring Vietnam as a Navy correspondent and artist were exhibited at the Smithsonian Institution in Washington, DC. The following year, National Geographic sent him to Barbados to document a historic sailing expedition.

Barnett subsequently created a series of Revolutionary War drawings and historical designs for the Franklin Mint. The designs included fifty medals for a chronology of the American Indian and several cachets for a Northwest Indian Mask series.

Toward the end of his life, Barnett completed a series of Southwestern landscapes. "If you're going to paint in the Southwest," he told his art students, "get a piano stool and put it out in the desert. Stay on that stool, because you can spend the rest of your life just painting the sky."

Order Form

Quantity	Amount
_____ One World, Many People ($19.95)	_____
Sales tax of 7.8 % for New Mexico residents	_____
Shipping and handling ($5.00 for first book Priority Mail; $3.00 for first book Media Mail; $1.00 for each additional book)	_____
Total amount enclosed	_____

Quantity discounts available

Method of payment

❐ Check or money order enclosed (made payable to **Young Scholars Press** in US funds only)

❐ MasterCard   ❐ VISA

CREDIT CARD # _____ EXP _____

SIGNATURE _____

Ship to (please print):

NAME _____

ADDRESS _____

CITY/STATE/ZIP _____

PHONE _____

YOUNG SCHOLARS PRESS
354 1/2 Calle Loma Norte, Santa Fe, NM 87501
phone 505-989-7116   fax 505-820-2367
www.oneworldmanypeople.com